J.O.Y.

DOC MURPHY

J.O.Y.

overcoming depression, fear, worry, and hopelessness

J.O.Y.

overcoming depression, fear, worry, and hopelessness

Doc Murphy

Doc Murphy Movements

Plano, Texas

Copyright © 2024 by Doc Murphy.

All rights reserved. No part of this book may be reproduced or transmitted in any form or by any means, electronic or mechanical, including photocopying, recording, or by any information storage and retrieval system, without permission in writing from the copyright owner.

Unless otherwise indicated all scripture quotations are taken from the King James Version of the bible.

Some scripture quotations are the author's paraphrase.

This book was printed in the United States of America.

Doc Murphy Movements
2220 Coit Rd. Ste 480-123
Plano, Tx. 75075

ISBN: 9798301660207

Published by Creative Apostle Everywhere / Everywhere Publishing, Plano, Tx.

For Booking and to order additional copies of this book, contact:

Doc Murphy Movements
pastordocmurphy@gmail.com
www.docmurphy.net

CONTENTS

INTRODUCTION: 5

1 If You Want to Experience Joy..........................8

2. Maximum Joy...15

3. Five Ways to Overcome Depression..................22

ABOUT THE AUTHOR...............28

PRODUCTS............................ 29

INTRODUCTION

Feeling overwhelmed by the trials of life? You're not alone. Challenges like depression, sickness, loneliness, hopelessness, fear, or financial hardship can weigh heavily on us. But I want you to know something powerful and unchanging: God desires to help you. He has all the strength, mercy, and grace you need for every trial or tribulation.

The Bible reminds us in **Hebrews 4:16**, *"Let us therefore come boldly unto the throne of grace, that we may obtain mercy, and find grace to help in time of need."* This promise is not distant or theoretical—it's for you, here and now.

What if, instead of being consumed by life's challenges, you could experience the transformative joy of Christ? His power and love have the ability to fill your heart with hope, encourage your spirit, and equip you with strength that defies circumstances.

The Joy OF the Lord

Let's pause and consider this phrase: "The joy **OF** the Lord is your strength." The word "of" is possessive. *It means that this joy belongs to someone—God Himself.* What's incredible is that this joy isn't just His to keep. He invites us to share in it, to make it our own. Imagine that—Jesus wants you to **own joy**!

Nehemiah 8:10 (NLT) says, *"Don't be dejected and sad, for the joy of the LORD is your strength!"* This joy is the kind that sustains and empowers. It's not based on fleeting happiness or external circumstances. It's rooted in the eternal, unchanging character of God.

We need the Lord's joy—not just any joy, but His. Why? Because the joy He gives makes us complete and whole. Jesus said in **John 15:11**, *"I have told you these things so that **_My joy may be in you_** and _your joy may be complete_."*

Today, take a bold step: ask Jesus for His joy. Let Him fill the broken and weary places of your life with His strength. You'll discover that His joy doesn't just get you through—it transforms everything.

Now, let's dive into the lesson and learn how to truly walk in the joy of the Lord!

Chapter One: If You Want to Experience JOY, You Need To…

J: Join in on the Kingdom of God

The Kingdom of God is a kingdom of joy. This joy is not superficial or dependent on what happens around us; it's a deep, abiding reality found in God's Spirit.

Romans 14:17 says, "For the kingdom of God is not eating and drinking, but righteousness and peace and joy in the Holy Spirit."

What makes this joy so extraordinary is its origin. It comes from God's Kingdom—a realm of righteousness, peace, and joy that transcends the world's struggles. When Jesus said in

Luke 17:21, "The kingdom of God is within you," He revealed something

9 | J.O.Y.

profound. If you've accepted Christ, His Kingdom is alive inside of you.

This Kingdom isn't earthly or temporal. Jesus made it clear in *John 18:36 when He said, "My kingdom is not of this world." And yet, this Kingdom has come to us!*

Colossians 1:13 says, "He has rescued us from the dominion of darkness and brought us into the kingdom of His beloved Son." As believers, we've been transferred from a kingdom of darkness into a culture of light, hope, and joy.

The culture of the Kingdom changes how we live. Culture is about language, behavior, and values. In the Kingdom, the fruits of the Spirit—love, joy, peace, patience, kindness, goodness, and faithfulness—become our new way of life (Galatians 5:22-23).

But here's the challenge: too often, we align ourselves with the world's system instead of the Kingdom. The world offers a culture of fear, anxiety, and despair. The Kingdom brings peace, love, and JOY.

Romans 12:2 tells us, "Do not conform to the pattern of this world, but be transformed by the renewing of your mind." When you embrace Kingdom living, joy becomes your reality.

O: Optimize Your Time with Thanksgiving and Wisdom

One reason people lose joy is they don't know how to be content. Contentment is a Kingdom virtue that protects us from bad decisions, debt, and worry.

Paul says in Philippians 4:11, "I have learned to be content whatever the circumstances." Learning contentment doesn't mean you stop believing God for greater things. It means you trust Him while waiting for the full manifestation of His promises.

When we lack contentment, we're prone to comparing ourselves to others, leading to frustration and depression. Worse, we start making decisions to impress others rather than obeying God. Remember, you're not in competition with anyone!

1 Timothy 6:6 reminds us, "Godliness with contentment is great gain." Instead of complaining or striving, thank God for what you already have. A thankful heart is fertile ground for joy to grow.

Y: Yield to the Holy Spirit

Yielding is about surrender. **It means giving up your own methods and trusting the Holy Spirit's guidance.** To yield is to present yourself to God, ready to follow His direction.

Galatians 5:16 says, "As you yield to the dynamic life and power of the Holy Spirit, you will abandon the cravings of your self-life." The Spirit leads us into joy, peace, and freedom, but we must let Him take the lead.

Think of a yield sign on the road. It means you slow down, let others pass, and proceed with caution. Spiritually, yielding means slowing down to hear God's voice, stepping aside to let Him lead, and following His path instead of your own.

We quench, resist, and grieve the Spirit when we fail to yield:

- ***Quench not*** the Spirit (1 Thessalonians 5:19): Don't suppress or ignore His voice.
- ***Resist not*** the Spirit (Acts 7:51): Don't push back against His leading.
- ***Grieve not*** the Spirit (Ephesians 4:30): Don't cause sorrow through

sin, disobedience, or unforgiveness.

When you yield to the Holy Spirit, you allow Him to produce the fruit of joy in your life. You stop striving in your own strength and start walking in the Spirit's power.

Summary

If you want to experience joy, you must:

1. Join in the Kingdom of God: Embrace Kingdom culture and let God's Spirit shape your life.
2. Optimize your time: Be content, thankful, and wise with what you have.
3. Yield to the Holy Spirit: Let Him lead, guide, and fill you with His dynamic power.

Joy isn't something you chase—it's a gift you receive when you align your heart with God's ways. Let's keep moving forward and discover more about this transforming joy!

Chapter Two: Maximum Joy

At all times—and in every season except during genuine tragedies—Christians should be the happiest people alive. Why? Because our joy is not rooted in circumstances; it is deeply anchored in God's Kingdom, promises, and Spirit.

James 1:2-4 (NKJV):
"My brethren, count it all joy when you fall into various trials, knowing that the testing of your faith produces patience. But let patience have its perfect work, that you may be perfect and complete, lacking nothing."

In the Berkeley translation, it says, *"Consider it maximum joy."* Imagine facing life's difficulties not with dread, but with a confident and even joyful anticipation of what God (His Word) is doing behind the scenes as we put the Word to practice.

What is Maximum Joy?

- **Joy:** Delight, exhilaration, gladness, and rejoicing.
- **Maximum:** ***The highest or greatest amount possible, extreme joy.***

We are accustomed to being happy when life is good. But as citizens of the Kingdom of God, we are called to go beyond that. Our joy doesn't depend on external factors—it is supernatural. The world can't comprehend it because this joy doesn't originate from the world.

Living Above the Norm

In today's culture, it's almost fashionable to say, "I'm not okay." But I'm here to tell you that it's OKAY TO BE OKAY! You're supposed to be OKAY! People gravitate toward negativity, airing problems with no solutions, and sinking into gloom. But in the Kingdom, we are ***normalizing joy, victory, and hope!*** We are redefining what's normal:

- **Normal is faith-filled living.**
- **Normal is finding joy in every trial.**
- **Normal is counting every challenge as an opportunity for maximum joy!**

"Count it all joy."
Paul's directive in James 1:2 isn't mere encouragement—it's a command. Why? Because every test from the enemy is a chance for God to show His faithfulness.

1 Peter 1:6 (NKJV):
"In this, you greatly rejoice, though now for a little while, if need be, you have been grieved by various trials."

Joy becomes our response to trials because we trust in God's deliverance. We count every problem as an **opportunity to rejoice**.

Why Can We Have Maximum Joy?

1. **God knows how to deliver us.**
   "The Lord knows how to deliver

the godly out of temptations..." (2 Peter 2:9).

2. **Our reward is certain.**
   "Blessed (happy) is the man who endures temptation..." (James 1:12).
   We find joy because we know our endurance leads to the crown of life.
3. **God delivers us from all troubles.**
   "Many are the afflictions of the righteous, but the Lord delivers him out of them all." (Psalm 34:19).
4. **The Holy Spirit fills us with joy.**
   Romans 14:17 reminds us that the Kingdom of God is *"righteousness, peace, and joy in the Holy Spirit."*

How Do We Tap Into This Joy?

1. **Be Filled with the Spirit.**
   "Do not be drunk on wine...but be filled with the Spirit." (Ephesians

5:18).
The Holy Spirit empowers us to rejoice even in the darkest times.
2. **Find Strength in His Joy.**
"The joy of the Lord is your strength." (Nehemiah 8:10).
3. **Embrace Contentment.**
"I have learned the secret of being content...I can do all things through Christ who strengthens me." (Philippians 4:12-13).

Viktor Frankl's Attitude Lesson

The Holocaust survivor Viktor Frankl wrote about how even in the darkest circumstances, *the last human freedom is the ability to choose one's attitude*. He discovered contentment even in suffering because he clung to hope and purpose.

Contentment is not complacency. It's the ability to rejoice in the waiting, trusting that God is faithful to His promises.

God's Word Brings Joy

<u>Instead of grieving over what the enemy says, celebrate what God has spoken.</u>

- *"I rejoice in Your Word like one who discovers great treasure."* (Psalm 119:162).

<u>Your celebration demonstrates your expectation</u>. If you truly expect God to fulfill His Word, your attitude will reflect joy, not doubt or despair.

Normalize Joy and Victory

It's time to redefine "normal" in our lives.

- **Normal is rejoicing in the Word.**
- **Normal is walking by faith, not feelings.**
- **Normal is choosing joy in the face of adversity.**

Sadness, fear, and gloom are not fruits of expectation. Instead, joy is the bridge between believing and receiving.

Psalm 119:111:
"Your testimonies are my heritage forever, for they are the joy of my heart."

So, let's reject the lies of the enemy that sorrow is inevitable. Let's normalize joy, normalize praise, and normalize victory. Because as believers, we walk by faith, and that means living in **maximum joy!**

Chapter Three: 5 Ways to Overcome Depression

Depression Defined:
Depression is a persistent feeling of sadness that impacts how you feel, think, and behave. It can lead to emotional and physical challenges, but there is hope and help in God's Word.

1. Identify the Root Cause

Understanding why depression has taken hold is critical. Is it due to ***disobedience, unresolved sin, or a distorted self-view***? When you have sin in your life, you will not have peace and if you don't have peace, you will become depressed. Saul, Israel's first king, **<u>battled depression because he disobeyed God</u>**. His rebellion caused the Spirit of the Lord to depart, leaving him jealous and tormented (1 Samuel 16:23).

Steps to Address the Root Cause:

- **Repent:** If disobedience has opened the door to depression, turn back to God (2 Chronicles 7:14).
- **Refocus Your Thoughts:** Stop dwelling on your past failures or perceived inadequacies (Numbers 13:33). Instead, meditate on your new identity in Christ (2 Corinthians 5:17).
- **Hope in God:** Redirect misplaced expectations. Stop relying on people to be what only God can be (Psalms 42:11; Psalms 62:5).

2. Speak to Your Soul

Like the psalmist, talk to your soul when it feels cast down or restless. Remind yourself to hope in God and praise Him despite your feelings (Psalm 42:11). Depression thrives when despair takes over, but faith can redirect your emotions.

Key Scriptures to Declare Over Your Soul:

- **Psalm 43:5:** "Why are you in despair, my soul? And why are you restless within me? Wait for God; for I will again praise Him."
- **Psalm 62:5:** "My soul, wait thou only upon God; for my expectation is from him."

3. Serve Others and Stop Comparing

Depression often stems from focusing inward—comparing ourselves to others, envying their success, or feeling unworthy. God calls us to look outward, serve others, and consider them more important than ourselves (Philippians 2:3-4).

Practical Actions:

- **Stop Competing:** Instead of trying to outdo others, outdo yourself in honoring them (Romans 12:10).

- **Celebrate Others' Successes:** Rejoice with those who rejoice (Romans 12:15).
- **Help Someone in Need:** Depression loses its grip when we focus on lifting others up.

4. Rejoice in Your Salvation

Sometimes depression arises because we forget the greatest reason to rejoice—our salvation. When King David lost his joy, he cried out, *"Restore to me the joy of your salvation"* (Psalm 51:12).

How to Reignite Your Joy in Salvation:

- **Praise God Daily:** Celebrate His faithfulness (Isaiah 61:3).
- **Meditate on His Word:** Find joy in His promises like one who discovers great treasure (Psalm 119:162).
- **Trust His Peace:** Jesus left us peace, not like the world's fleeting

comfort, but perfect and enduring peace (John 14:27).

5. Practice Gratitude and Contentment

Ungratefulness and discontentment can open the door to depression. When we focus on what we lack instead of what God has provided, we lose our peace.

Steps to Cultivate Contentment:

- **Thank God Daily:** Recognize and appreciate what you already have (1 Timothy 6:6-8).
- **Stop Complaining:** Complaints stir God's anger and harden the heart (Numbers 11:1).
- **Be Content in Every Season:** Learn to find joy whether in abundance or need, trusting God for your future (Philippians 4:11-13).

Overcoming Depression Through Faith:
Depression may feel overwhelming, but it

is not invincible. By identifying the root cause, speaking truth to your soul, serving others, rejoicing in your salvation, and practicing gratitude, you can defeat the spirit of despair.

Nehemiah 8:10 reminds us: *"The joy of the Lord is your strength."* Choose joy today and let God's strength carry you through.

About the Author

Doc Murphy travels teaching the Word of Faith. He plants churches everywhere.

He is also the founder of Doc Murphy Movements/ The Everywhere Network a church planting organization. He is the author of several books and is an accomplished songwriter and music producer. For more information, log on to our website at www.docmurphy.net.

Other Books and Products by Doc Murphy

Five + One Series

Becoming The Balanced You

Favor is Fair

The Faith Strategy To Change A Nation

Frequency

YOU Success

The Green-Eyed Monster Game

Eagle Leaders

Producers

Nonnegotionables

S. I. Supernatural Intelligence

Dream Responsibly

The God of Increase

History Makers

Faith

Born for this

The Apostolic Church

Everywhere

Small Church, Large Church

Prayer Protocols

History Makers

Worship

Kingdompreneur

You are Exceptional

On A Mission

Go Ready Set!

Full Time Believing

Pioneer Leaders

How to get God to Hear You

DOCtrine: The Education of Peace Instrumental Album

Faithfull EP by Doc and Mary Murphy

Small Church Worship by Everywhere Worship

Order these products @ amazon.com

33 |J . O . Y .

Made in the USA
Columbia, SC
13 December 2024